D1245616

LA GOMERA

Island of Columbus · Unspoilt Gem of the Canaries

Photographs by
KRISTINE EDLE OLSEN

Text and captions by Caroline MacDonald-Haig

with 231 illustrations in colour, and 1 map

THAMES AND HUDSON
in association with A/S Toko

ACKNOWLEDGEMENTS

Many people helped us in preparing this book and we would like to thank particularly Abuelo y Abuela, Carmita, Manuel Lopez Mora, Virgilo Brito, Ellen von Rosen, Jan Stael von Holstein, Franka and Christian.

ABOVE *The island's armorial decorates the wall outside the Parador Nacional hotel on the headland above San Sebastián. On it are carved the honey-cups in which the* miel de palma *was traditionally carried, one for each important region of the island, at the time of the Condes (Counts) of Gomera.*
PAGE 1 *Homing pigeons,* palomas, *high in the sky over Playa de Santiago. Pigeon-racing is still a popular sport, and birds are taken across to Tenerife and released to fly home.*
PAGES 2/3 *Sunset over La Gomera, seen from Los Cristianos in Tenerife.*

Any copy of this book issued by the publisher as a paperback is sold subject to the condition that it shall not, by way of trade or otherwise. be lent, resold, hired our or otherwise circulated without the publisher's permission in any form of binding or cover other than that in which it is published and without a similar condition including these words being imposed on a subsequent purchaser.

© 1989 A/S Toko, Hvitsten

All rights reserved. No part of this publication may be reproduced or transmitted in any form or by any means, electronic or mechanical, including photocopy, recording or any other information storage and retrieval system without prior permission in writing from the publisher.

Printed and bound in Japan by Dai Nippon

CONTENTS

Young Gomeros in their fiesta finery.

Just 25 km south-west of Tenerife in the Canary archipelago lies the beautiful unspoiled island of La Gomera.

This island has been spared the ravages of modern mass-tourism and has retained its character: when viewed from the sea, the encircling basalt cliffs and crags make it appear quite inaccessible; and also, the island does not offer any of the immediately obvious tourist attractions; there are no long golden beaches, although there are some modest grey ones, and no airport either. Visitors who do make the 1½-hour ferry crossing from Tenerife are captivated by the beauty and variety of Gomera's hidden landscape, with its old villages and steep terraced mountainsides, and by its welcoming courteous people. This island is particularly appealing to those who enjoy remote places and love walking and bird-watching.

Between 2 and 20 million years ago, volcanic forces off the west coast of Africa formed the Canary archipelago with its seven main islands. Only on Gomera has there been no measurable volcanic activity since then, and time and erosion have given the island a rich and settled looking landscape. In the north there are several extraordinary cone-shaped outcrops (*roques*) which dominate the landscape and are thought to be the interior cones or vents of the volcanoes which erupted under the sea.

Gomera's size is deceptive; it measures at most only 22 km from north to south and 25 km from east to west, but because of its mountainous interior it can take hours to go from one side of the island to the other. From the central peak of Garajonay (1,487 m) steep-sided valleys, called *barrancos,* radiate outwards and tumble in jagged ranges to the sea. Softening the rugged landscape are the most wonderfully fertile terraced valleys which from early springtime are stippled with new cultivation; small plateaus of meadow grazed by sheep and goats clothe the lower slopes and by the sea is the emerald mantle of the banana plantations. Most unexpected of all is the dense subtropical rain forest, the greater part of which is now a national park, where tree heathers and native laurels predominate, and which cloaks the northern reaches of the mountains. Through its perfectly balanced ecosystem it is the island's surest source of water and continuing agricultural prosperity.

Gomera's hot climate averages 20°C in winter and 26° in summer, the heat of the sun being tempered by the trade winds blowing off the Atlantic. As they meet the north face of the mountains the moisture-laden air is cooled and forms a thick cloud cover to produce conditions in which the forest thrives. When these mountains are blanketed in cloud, the southern slopes, which are less steep, are bathed in sunshine, the result being a great variety of vegetation – desert-like and sparse in the south, green and lush in the north. On cloudless days, the forest shimmers with green-filtered sunlight and is strangely cool and dim after the glaring heat outside.

To this fortunate island came early man, probably around 3000 to 2500 BC, when the European neolithic culture was at its height. Opinions abound as to where precisely the first Gomeros came from, but most agree on North Africa: one distinguished anthropologist holds that the name Gomera may have come from a Berber tribe, the Gumara, which still exists in old Spanish Morocco; still another claims that inhabitants of Africa who lived in the mountains of Mauritania were called Gumeros or Gomerites and migrated to Gomera. Mummified remains found in caves suggest, tenuously, links with ancient Egypt too.

Like the rest of the Canaries, Gomera was visited throughout antiquity by Egyptian, Phoenician, Carthaginian and Roman ships – fragments of amphorae have been found on the sea bed – and Plutarch in his 'Life of Sertorius' refers to the islands as the 'Isles of the Blessed, . . . with a good rich soil bearing abundant wild fruits sufficient to nourish an idle people . . . even among the barbarians [there is] the firm belief that these are the Elysian Fields, the dwelling place of the blessed of which Homer sang.' After being shown on the outer edge of Ptolemy's world map in the 2nd century AD, nothing more is known of Gomera for a thousand years.

The town of Playa de Santiago in the 1920s. Methods of sowing and harvesting have changed little over the years.

Torre del Conde. The only medieval building of its type in the Canaries, erected c. 1450 by the Castilian Hernán Peraza. A century and a half later, it was to be a bastion against pirates.

Varied agriculture provides the ingredients for a delicious and unusual local cuisine.

At the end of the 13th century, slave traders came, and later the Genoese, Portuguese, Dutch, French and Castilians. For the first half of the 15th century both Portuguese and Castilians had rival claims to Gomera. In 1445, the Castilian Hernán Peraza, later Count of Gomera, bought the rights to the island from one Don Guillén de Las Casas, son of an influential slave trader, and built his fortress, the Torre del Conde, which still stands by the sea in San Sebastián, the island's capital. His grandson, Hernán Peraza the younger, treated the Gomeros with such brutality that they plotted against him and in 1487 he was lured to his death at Degollada de Peraza, just west of the town. His widow, the equally perfidious Beatriz de Bobadilla, formerly mistress of King Ferdinand of Aragon, became ruler of Gomera, and it was she who welcomed Christopher Columbus when he came to provision his ships in San Sebastián in 1492 before sailing to America.

Columbus' visit is the most important event in the island's history: consequently, Gomera is often referred to as 'La Isla Colombina'. Later the harbour sheltered both Cortez and Pizarro, and ships of the Armada fleet were repaired here with timber from the forest. So strategic was it that in 1743 the English Admiral Charles Windham was sent with a small fleet to take the town. He was beaten off, however, and in the Church of the Assumption there is a splendid, if somewhat peeling, mural painted in 1760 depicting the victory.

The people whom the European seafarers found on the islands were the Guanches; the name is thought to be derived from the aboriginals' own word for man. Skulls preserved in burial caves reveal a people with squarish heads and prominent brow lines; records state that they had frizzy red hair and blue eyes. Until the 15th century the culture was still that of the Stone Age. The people were cave-dwellers who grew cereals, tended livestock and took from the sea whatever they could reach from the shore: recent erosion at Arguamul in the north-west has revealed layers of limpet shells 3 m below the present level of the village. From the forest they obtained wood for cooking and making weapons. They trained their youths to be agile by making them dodge clay balls and rocks thrown at them. They worshipped nature and through their practice of embalming the dead they evidently believed in an afterlife. Elements of Guanche life are still very much alive today. The local pottery is so ancient in design that archaeologists compare it with that of the Middle East *c.* 3000 BC, and traditional ceramic wares continue to be made in El Cercado; *el silbo,* their unique piercing whistle language, is used in the mountains by farmers and shepherds to call to each other across the rugged *barrancos*; and the shepherds use the *astia,* a 3 m-long pole pointed at one end, to swing themselves up and down the mountainsides. Place names and nouns beginning with 'Be', 'Ch', 'T' or 'Gua' are evidence of their pre-Hispanic origins; for example, Benchijigua, a village below Roque de Agando, *guarapo*, the palm-tree sap which is made into the most delicious syrup, *miel de palma* (literally, 'palm honey').

The last years of the 15th century were not happy ones for the Guanches, who were heavily taxed, and regarded by the island's conquerors as a legitimate source of revenue as slaves. They were also made to pay horribly for the death of Peraza. They were defended before the Castilian courts by two successive bishops and within two or three generations the two sides had settled down together. Christianity became the integrating force.

The earliest Christian presence in the island is the little *ermita* at Tazo, said to have been built by Portuguese sailors shipwrecked on the treacherous rocks off the north-western coast in 1414. Later, Castilian conquistadors destroyed the old pagan place of worship and the fortress at Fortaleza, poisoning the well there, and built the first church at nearby Chipude. There are many examples of isolated little *ermitas*, and in each town there is a substantial church decorated with richly carved retables and statues of saints. In each church will be found a tender and expressive life-size statue of the Virgin, often gorgeously arrayed in velvet and lace. The devoutly Catholic people of Gomera venerate especially Our Lady of Guadalupe, the island's patroness. Most of the *ermitas* and churches are the focus of an annual fiesta which the Gomeros celebrate with great enthusiasm and with a good deal of singing and dancing, poetry and feasting. These celebrations are famous throughout the Canaries.

The island's economy, based on agriculture and fishing, has improved greatly as a result of the introduction of a road system and (since 1974) of the regular ferry service to Tenerife. During the present century thousands of Gomeros have emigrated to Cuba, Venezuela, mainland Spain and, more recently, to Tenerife; the population, which has dwindled from *c.* 30,000 in 1940 to *c.* 18,000 today, is now about the same as it was in 1900.

Government administration is centred on Tenerife, but Gomera's interests are overseen by the Cabildo Insular, the Island Council, based in San Sebastián. The island itself is divided up into *ayuntamientos*, or municipal districts, each of which, with the exception of Valle Gran Rey, takes its name from the principal town in the region. The plan of this book is to take as our starting point the capital, San Sebastián, in the south-east, and then to explore the rest of the island district by district in clockwise fashion (see map, p.128).

The statue of the Virgin in the church of Alajeró is greatly revered by the local people.

FURTHER READING

Landscapes of Southern Tenerife & La Gomera, by Noel Rochford (Sunflower Books, London), 1988. Pocket guide to walks on the island, with detailed maps.

What's Blooming Where on Tenerife?, by Hubert Moeller (Bambi, Puerto de la Cruz, Tenerife), 1968. Much of the flora of La Gomera is also found on neighbouring Tenerife, and this book, published in English and German editions, provides an excellent guide.

The only good histories of La Gomera available are in Spanish. They include: *Episodios Gomeros del Siglo XV* by José Trujillo Cabrera (Ediciones Gráficas Tenerife, Santa Cruz de Tenerife), 1969; and *Lugares Colombinos de la Villa de San Sebastián* by Alberto Darias Principe (Cabildo Insular de La Gomera, San Sebastián), 1986.

(LEFT, ABOVE AND BELOW) *Vicente Paz Montecino, Castro Montecino Simanca, Merchor Chinea and their workmates rest from their labours in the banana plantation at Playa de Santiago.*
(ABOVE) *El Negro demonstrates the technique of the Gomeros' whistle language,* el silbo. (BELOW) *This is a haven for local children.*

10

People of La Gomera

Hard work does not dampen the spirits of women like Modesta Chinea (TOP LEFT), Carolina Arzola Arzola (TOP RIGHT) and Antonia Negrini (CENTRE). (ABOVE) Cristina. (RIGHT) An old man wends his way home with his goat.

SAN SEBASTIAN

The historic centre of the island's capital, San Sebastián, lies at the bottom of the wide Barranco de la Villa, commanding one of the finest natural harbours in the Canaries.

San Sebastián was for long an important port of call for ships en route from Europe to the New World: every navigator and every conquistador used it; Cortez and Pizarro, Magellan and Amerigo Vespucci took on supplies and had their ships repaired here. And so it remained for 300 years after Columbus. The earliest buildings date from the 15th century. There are five of particular historic interest and all would have been known to Columbus. The most striking is the Torre del Conde. The others are in the Calle del Medio, one minute's walk from the port across the central Plaza de los Descubridores. The first house is where Columbus drew water for the 1492 expedition. Further up on the right is the gothic Church of the Assumption; built in 1490 and greatly enlarged a few years later, it is the place where Columbus knelt to ask God's blessing for the voyage ahead. Inside the shadows exhale centuries of sweet incense. The carving of the wooden screens and ceilings is well worth looking at; just inside the main door is a magnificent sinuous lattice wall studded with flowers, and the star-spangled coffered vault above the Retablo del Pilar is enchanting. Beyond the church is the restored Casa de Colón, where Columbus stayed; it is a perfect example of the colonial island style, with heavy wooden shutters and an interior courtyard. A few steps further up the

[*continued on page 17*]

San Sebastián, with Tenerife beyond.

In the centre of the old town there are a few architectural surprises: elaborate 19th-century Spanish baroque (ABOVE LEFT) sits alongside the older town houses, unadorned except for their panelled shutters and lattice balconies.

(OPPOSITE) *Looking north up the Barranco de la Villa to where the main roads, the Carretera del Norte and the Carretera del Centro, leave the town.*

street is the primitive Ermita de San Sebastián.

All along this street, through open doorways, you can glimpse small courtyards bright with greenery and filled with bird-song; 'típico Canario,' comments a passing Gomero, waving at the caged songbirds. He is right. Such leafy domestic oases are to be found all over the island, and it is the only place to see the domestic golden-plumed Canary bird.

Modern, and mostly 20th-century, San Sebastián has spread up the sides of the *barranco*. Two main roads link the capital with the rest of the island. Near the port in the Plaza de America, are the offices of the Island Council and the public library. Built only a few years ago in an attractive Canarian style with arcades, balconies and wrought-iron grilles, these buildings show a concern for design that was almost completely absent in the early 1970s when this dignified little town was in danger of being swamped with concrete boxes.

In the bars and cafés, restaurants and the few boutiques which cluster round the central plaza, shaded by huge laurel trees, the atmosphere is quite cosmopolitan, but the countryside is never far away. At the edges of the town, ten minutes' walk away, are small farms, and on the main road into the town it is common to see women carrying enormous bundles of grass on their heads to feed their animals.

The region of San Sebastián is dry and covers the south-east corner of the island. There is a scattering of villages and hamlets, watered by the complex network of irrigation canals and pipes which snake along beside the roads and over the mountains. You can walk to the little coves and beaches hidden at the bottom of the *barrancos* that indent the coastline.

Old windmill on the edge of San Sebastián.

Mural in the north aisle of the Church of the Assumption, painted in 1760 in gratitude for the victory granted to Don Diego Bueno in 1743, when he repulsed the attack by the English naval force under Admiral Charles Windham.

The ferry Gomera leaving the harbour. A cruise ship is tied up at the quayside.

Columbus's well. The notice on the lid records that water from this well was used to baptize America.

(OPPOSITE) The Church of the Assumption, where Columbus prayed, and the lighthouse at Punta de San Cristóbal.

In the Church of the Assumption the statue of the Virgen del Pilar (TOP) adorns the central Retablo del Rosario, *and that of the Archangel Michael stands in a fantastically carved and marbled retable.*

20

Good Friday procession in San Sebastián.

21

Desert-loving plants, the prickly pear
and tabaiba, a bushy euphorbia, clothe
the mountainside above La Laja.
(OPPOSITE) Pine trees grow on the
fringes of the forest at La Laja.

(LEFT) *View from Jerduñe down the* barranco.
(ABOVE) *A caterpillar feeding, and a rooftop with old tiles, mossed by time, on the road to Seima.*

It was from hamlets like Seima, in the driest regions of the island where life was frequently threatened by drought, that many Gomeros emigrated to Cuba or Venezuela. Following heavier than usual winter rains the mountains are carpeted in green.

(ABOVE) *House built into the cliff above Seima.* (BELOW) *A pathetic scattering of personal belongings abandoned for the prospect of a less harsh life on the Peninsula (Spain) or on Tenerife.*

Barranco Juán de Vera, above Playa del Cabrito.

Old houses and the watermill (ABOVE RIGHT) *in Benchijigua.*

Roque de Agando
wreathed in mist above
Benchijigua.

One of the giant eucalyptus trees
which grow beside the path leading
into Benchijigua.
Conical hill near Jerduñe covered
with aloe and tabaiba.
(OPPOSITE) *Track from Benchijigua,
crowned by the Roque de Agando
which dominates the skyline.*

Palm trees whose ragged trunks show
where they have been cut for harvesting guarapo – *the sap from which the
rich syrupy* miel de palma *is made.*
(OPPOSITE) *View from Lo del Gato down
the* barranco, *looking towards the south.*

Wild Flowers

The wild flowers on Gomera are spectacular, especially in early spring. Many like the golden sempervivum (lower far left) or white eupatorium (top left) are indigenous to the Canaries. They are very varied too: the robust plants which thrive in the heat and drought of the south, such as the abundant tabaiba (far right), seen here in flower, are quite different from those which need adequate moisture to flourish.

ALAJERO

Contrary to the norm, the small town of Alajeró is not set in a valley. Instead, it stands on the south-facing slopes of a mountain, 9 km from the sea. This is one of the oldest towns on the island, as can be seen from the church and the small houses which huddle round it. It is a hot, dry district but in springtime the newly ploughed red earth on the hillsides soon sprouts green, and the region is known for its grain crops and for its almond and fig trees. This is a quiet, sleepy town and at siesta time nothing disturbs the silence except the continual low hum of bees and the scuttering of lizards as they start through the undergrowth. The climate is obviously healthy, as a visit to the local cemetery, with its ranks of long boxes into which the coffins are pushed, will tell you: the devoutly tended memorials to long-lived local people record great ages like 89, 107, 85, 95. The working life here may be hard, but it certainly doesn't seem stressful.

There is a *gofio* mill here where people still bring their own home-grown grain, previously roasted at home, to be ground into the light caramel-coloured flour which was formerly one of the Guanches' staple foods. After a day's milling the town is afloat with the sweet aroma of roasted corn.

The sea round the Alajeró coastline is rich in fish, and one of the region's main sources of income is fishing off Playa de Santiago. The fishermen return very early in the morning, and by midday all traces of their labours have been swept away, except perhaps for a stray fish-head buzzing with glittering metallic-green flies and a nacreous scattering of fish-scales. The catch is taken to Tenerife by ferry in refrigerated lorries.

The terrain here is dramatic; to the south-west is the rounded peak of El Calvario crowned with its little chapel, and to the north is the immense gorge of Imada. In order to obtain the best view of the village of Imada, cradled in its *barranco*, take the road north out of Alajeró and then the right-hand turn to the village, which is clearly signposted. Beyond, on the far rim of the gorge, is a ragged tree-line and the faintest wisp of mist; this is the first glimpse of the rain forest when approached from the arid south. It is a long, but exhilarating walk down this gorge to the sea at Playa de Santiago.

(OPPOSITE) *The west façade of the old church and* (ABOVE LEFT) *the ornate retable behind the altar.* (BELOW LEFT) *View looking south over the cemetery wall; here are to be found many memorials like the one shown here* (CENTRE LEFT).

Life in Alajeró involves little stress.

(OPPOSITE) *The threshing floor at Las Toscas* (TOP). *Maize, which with barley and wheat is most commonly used in making* gofio, *is dried in the sun* (BELOW).

Many Gomeros still grow and roast their own grain to make gofio. *Often the grain is delivered to the mill in marked bags to ensure that each family gets back their own special blend.*

(TOP LEFT AND ABOVE) *Ramón Trujillo and Teresa García at work in the* gofio *mill.* (CENTRE LEFT) *The blend of maize, barley and wheat is roasted in a large shallow dish over the fire and stirred constantly to prevent burning.* (LEFT) *Workers take* gofio *with them for lunch, carried in a crude goat- or sheep-skin bag. When hungry, they add liquid to the flour and knead it in the skin till the mixture has the consistency of stiff dough. They break it off in lumps and eat it – delicious.*

(OPPOSITE) *House in Targa, on the road from Playa de Santiago to Alajeró,
with Mount Teide on Tenerife as a backcloth.*
(ABOVE) *House outside Alajeró, and a view from the road between Alajeró
and Garajonay.*

A magnificent tethered billy goat surveys his territory; and a herdsman, with his astia *on his shoulder, takes the easy route.*

The early evening feed outside Alajeró.

Roque de Agando seen in silhouette from Imada.

Vine trellis on the edge of a terrace.

Old houses in Imada.

Cochineal insects cause the mouldy patches on the prickly pear – in the mid-19th century the insects were grown and harvested for the red dye they yielded, and were an important cash crop.

(OPPOSITE) *Imada, at the head of the* barranco, *with an almond tree in the foreground.*

Looking north to Imada on the left and Benchijigua on the right.
There are good tracks to follow in the Imada gorge (INSETS), but they are steep and stony

(LEFT) *Playa de Santiago seen from the sea. Because there was very little water available, there were no houses here until the beginning of this century; just a few people lived in caves in the cliffs which shelter the harbour. Some of these caves are still used to house animals and as store rooms, and at the western end of the quay a restaurant has been built into one of them – its crazy jagged rock ceiling hung with baskets of ferns makes an original interior. Immaculate little bars and cafés sell fish and are topically decorated with fishing nets festooned with starfish, fishing floats and old fish-hooks. The harbour wall makes this a safe anchorage, and the sand and pebble beach is a favourite spot for local children to swim. There are a few pensions here overlooking the sea.*

(BELOW) *On the cliff-top above the eastern arm of Playa de Santiago is the new village-like Hotel Tecina in its lush garden setting.*

Playa de Santiago.
Mount Teide on Tener-
ife, over 35 km away,
rises beyond the cliffs.

Sunrise over the sea.

Grey-black pebbles on the shore reveal the volcanic origins of Gomera.

(LEFT) *Large water-worn pebbles piled up on the beach.*
(ABOVE) *Poinsettias, otherwise known as Christmas Stars, blown by the winter winds, and a view of the cemetery at Playa de Santiago.*
(OPPOSITE) *Old palm trees with gnarled trunks are evidence of past harvests of* guarapo.

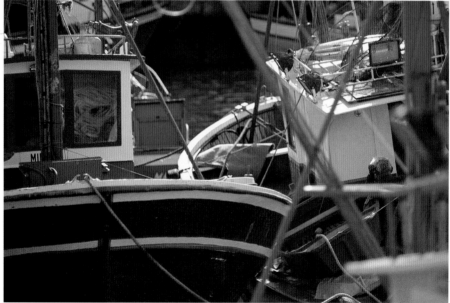

Outside a cottage door a colourful array of washing is hung out to dry. The local people are artists with their boats, the decorative flourishes are as important as the protection the fresh paint provides against the strong sun, which would soon cause bare timbers to shrink.

Sitting in the shade of a giant laurel tree at a seafront bar.

(OVERLEAF) *The sun setting over Playa de Santiago.* >

(FAR LEFT) *Looking down into Erquito from the road to La Dama.*

Poppies in the corn.

Old roof edged with stones to anchor the tiles in winter storms.

La Dama with Fortaleza in the distance.
Abandoned fish factory at La Rajita.

(RIGHT) *Even the steepest valleys like the Barranco de La Rajita are ridged with old terraces built in seemingly inaccessible places.*

(LEFT) *Inshore fishing close to the rocky coast. Among the varieties of fish caught in the waters around La Gomera and the other islands of the Canary archipelago are sardines, mackerel, tuna and swordfish.*
(RIGHT) *Bananas and citrus fruit are particularly suited to the Gomera climate. The Canary banana,* Musa cavendishii, *produces a bunch weighing about 28 kg.*

(BELOW, LEFT) El silbo, *the Gomeros' traditional whistle language, is still used by some farmers and herdsmen to call to each other across the* barrancos; *by placing his fingers (in various combinations) in his mouth, a skilled* silbador *can produce a wide range of notes which can be clearly distinguished and interpreted at a distance. Domingo Cabello, who shows his skills here, is also seen leaping expertly with the aid*

of his astia. *The rough, rocky, terrain (below, centre) is typical of the countryside where herdsmen graze their goats and sheep.*

(BELOW RIGHT) *Goat's- and sheep's-milk cheese made in the villages is often traded in the local* tiendas *(shops). Clotilde Torres fills the mould with curd.*

Pigs have a special place in the Gomero's heart, and in the more remote districts killing and preparing the pig is a traditional ceremony involving family and friends. It starts at sunrise with the men killing the pig and singeing its hairs over the fire. Then it is butchered. By evening, when almost every part of the animal has been carefully preserved in some way or other, much wine will have been drunk as an accompaniment to gofio mixed with chicharrón, the delicious roast titbits left after rendering.

VALLE GRAN REY

Valle Gran Rey has a mannered, cultivated beauty not to be found anywhere else on the island. The well-kept terraces, watered by springs and conduits from mountain reservoirs, are astonishingly green and completely cover the sides and bottom of the magnificent *barranco*, which is the largest on Gomera. It was here that the first tourists came in the early 1970s. The conglomeration of small pensions that have been built close to the beaches tears at the hearts of those early visitors who remember the island as it was ten or twenty years ago, when the winding road led only to the sea.

The name, meaning 'valley of the great king', almost certainly derives from the Guanche King Hupalupa who with his son plotted the assassination of Count Hernán Peraza to avenge the rape of the Princess Iballa. Legend has it that it was on La Baja del Secreto, a reef about 300 m from the shore, that the two plotted, and when Hupolupa's son asked, '...and if the Count hears about it?', his father replied, 'If he knows, it is because of you', and stabbed his son to death.

The seashore at Playa de Valle Gran Rey.

(ABOVE) *La Calera, at the bottom of Valle Gran Rey.*
(OPPOSITE) *Terraces in sinuous ranks climb the steep sides of the* barranco.
(FAR RIGHT) *Vertiginous rocks line the road leading from Arure down into
the valley.*

The road from San Sebastián to Valle Gran Rey passes through the small mountain villages of Igualero, Chipude and El Cercado, which belong in the southern sector of Vallehermoso (pages 80-107).
(OPPOSITE) *Pines at Igualero, near the edge of the forest.*
(ABOVE) *Almond blossom in El Cercado, and palm trees frame the distant mountain village of Chipude.*

(RIGHT) *The* mesa *('table') of Fortaleza, above Chipude (see previous page), was sacred to the Guanches, who called it Argodey. On the flat top are the remains of a double circle of boulders with a central menhir and traces of a megalithic culture dating from c. 3000-2000 BC.*

(ABOVE) *Clotilde Mesa Ortíz, 86, from Chipude, tells a story; and Antonio Ortíz stands in the family wine-press in Chipude.*

In the early 15th century, at the beginning of the historic period, Gomera was divided into four territories, and the head was the ancient mountain village of Arure with its old stone houses (ABOVE) half-hidden among palm groves. The name derives from 'Aruri', a Berber word meaning the 'king's house' or the 'paternal lineage'. (LEFT) After good winter rains the swollen rivers cascade down the falls. (RIGHT) A cave entrance provides beehives with shelter from the fierce westerly winds.

The wind blowing from the Atlantic has eroded the rocks at Taguluche into
bleak sentinels.
(OPPOSITE) Sheer basalt cliffs enclose the barranco above Taguluche.

Garden Flowers and Shrubs

Around every house flowers and shrubs grow in profusion, planted in all manner of containers – plastic buckets, oil drums, old cooking pots, detergent bottles – nothing is too humble to be pressed into service. Some exotic trees like the Australian fire acacia (TOP LEFT) shade village houses.

VALLEHERMOSO

Doors and windows closed against the sun at siesta time.

Of all the towns on the island, this one, set in a long winding valley away from the sea, has a bustling provincial atmosphere. Entering from the north, along the Carretera del Norte, the first thing that comes into sight is the wild monolith of the Roque Cano which towers over the town. To the right is a smaller road which goes along the river to the sea. Here is cultivation of a different kind, bamboo, a crop which is almost as much an island staple as grain or potatoes. It can be put to so many uses: trellises for the vineyards, fishing rods, birdcages, fencing and most of all as stakes for tomatoes. It grows abundantly in the river-bed where the noises are of soothing bird song and running water – quite different from the raucous dogs and chickens of the villages. At the end of the road is a beach, beguiling in the sunlight, but a dangerous place to swim because of powerful undercurrents and Atlantic swells.

At the northern end of the town the houses are set close together in a web of steep, narrow streets that lead onto the plaza in front of the big 19th-century gothic church. Shuttered windows and panelled doors keep out the heat, and little rooftop gardens grow onions in short rows edged with flowers. Because it is so difficult to move around the island, there is no tradition of open markets. Extra produce is often bartered with the local *tienda* which sells absolutely everything and is a good place to find village cheeses or bottles of palm syrup.

An arm of the rain forest bounds Vallehermoso on three sides and the clouds it attracts bring far more moisture to this region than the south. The sides of the valley are much greener and the villages of Alojera, Epina and Arguamal look lush and prosperous. Here are the finest of the palm groves for which La Gomera is famous, Vallehermoso being the main centre for making *miel de palma*, the sweet dark caramel-coloured syrup made from the palm-tree sap, *guarapo*. Traditionally the sweetener used by the Guanches, this palm syrup took the place of sugar in the Gomeros' cooking during World War II, when scarcely any ships came to these islands. It is particularly good eaten with *torta de cuajada*, a curd-cheese pancake. Palms tapped for *guarapo* can be recognized by the tin collar nailed halfway up the trunk to prevent vermin from climbing into the sap as it is collected.

(OPPOSITE) *A narrow street leading to the church.*

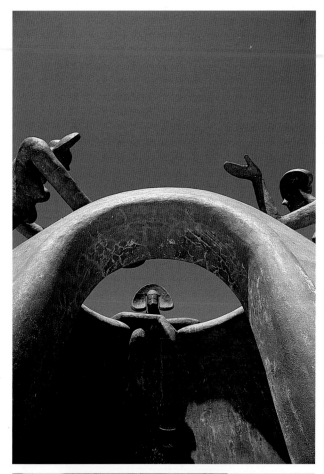

Voluptuous larger than life-size concrete figures adorn the play park in Vallehermoso.

Orencio Cabrera Valeriano, Pedro Carrea Marichal and Juán Chinea García relax in the plaza.

Amalia Moreno, 83, with her grandchildren.

(OPPOSITE) *Roque Cano sits brooding above the town* (ABOVE), *and old and new houses ascend the valley above the church.*

View from the road to Epina above Vallehermoso, with (INSETS) Playa de Vallehermoso and crops growing at the bottom of the valley.

(ABOVE) *Pathway leading to the famous springs, the Chorros de Epina, set in the shade of the forest just outside the village of Epina. The waters are channelled into hollowed-out branches.*
(LEFT) *Terraced cultivation at Epina.*

In every village chickens scratch by the roadside. The spiky plants seen here are aloes, which grow everywhere and were once an important ingredient in herbal medicines. Although this scene appears peaceful enough, the chickens are never silent. Distant villages, hidden from view by the mountains, can be located by the sounds of crowing cockerels and barking dogs, and outside the villages goat- and sheep-bells can be heard ringing across the barrancos.

The road from Alojera to the sea winds down to a grey-black beach where even the grass-hoppers have adapted to their environment and have become grey.

Rocky coastline south of Playa de Alojera.

*Alojera's black beach is clear evidence of the volcanic activity which cre-
ated Gomera millions of years ago.*

Alojera. The village is set on a wide open slope looking westward to the sea, overlooked by Montaña de Calvario, thought to have been another religious sanctuary of the Guanches.

Most new houses are built of cement blocks, rendered and painted white. At the rear is a bamboo fence.

Newly planted terraces.

Patterns of husbandry (CLOCKWISE FROM TOP LEFT). *Central irrigation channel is earthed up to allow water to run between rows of potatoes. Tomatoes trussed on bamboo frames. The edges of each irrigation channel are clearly marked with different plants, here it is rows of beans. Palm tree being tapped for* guarapo.

The road from Epina to Tazo follows the northern arm of the rain forest. It starts off in a green landscape where the air is scented with pines and the almond trees by the roadside are bearded with moss. As the road turns westward towards the sea, a desert mountain landscape takes over until suddenly the remote oasis of Tazo, with its palm-fringed cistern (OPPOSITE) comes into view. A few of the houses are still inhabited. Pepper trees shelter the patios, and women in black with huge shady hats tend their animals. In one farmhouse a disused bread oven has been converted to a dairy. On boards hung from the ceiling white rounds of cheese were set out to dry in the cool smoke-blackened interior. The cool of the farmhouse, with its thick stone walls, is very welcome in the heat of the day when nothing stirs except the dragonflies and butterflies, which dart and flutter over the rocks and in the palm groves. Just outside Tazo is the beautiful Ermita de Santa Lucía.

94

A sharp ridge of mountains separates Arguamul from Tazo (previous page). Arguamul is a flourishing mountain village at the end of a road which looks as if it leads nowhere.
(OPPOSITE) *Three views over the mountains from outside Arguamul.*

The mountains below Arguamul fall steeply to the sea, where treacherous rocks are constantly washed by heavy swell. (OPPOSITE) A dramatically sited farmhouse on the way to Arguamul.

*The vertical clusters of basalt which throw up their jagged fingers all over Gomera are at their most spectacular at Los Organos ('the organ pipes') in the very north of the island (*RIGHT AND OVERLEAF*). These extraordinary columnar formations can only be viewed by boat, best hired from La Calera in Valle Gran Rey, Playa de Santiago or San Sebastián.*

(BELOW) *Millions of years ago fresh injections of molten lava pushed aside previous layers of volcanic rock.*

Rugged landscape at Tamargada, on the northern edge of the rain forest.

Tamargada. Although many of the more inaccessible terraces like these are no longer worked, a surprising number within reach of a small diesel-powered cultivator or the trusty oxen are still ploughed and planted. (OPPOSITE) Old houses set in a palm grove, and (BELOW) stone terrace walls, which are repaired each year before spring planting.

106

AGULO

Without doubt Agulo is the prettiest town on the island. Its two centres, La Montañeta and Las Casas, crown the low-lying hilltop surrounded by banana plantations; behind it are the sheer cliffs of Bisquite and in front is the sea and the distant Mount Teide on Tenerife.

In recent years the local population has dwindled as a result of emigration, which means that Agulo has been spared the curse of many towns – modern development using concrete and preformed blocks. Here it is still possible to walk down narrow cobbled streets lined with old stone houses shuttered against the brilliant sun and, apart from a wrought-iron street lamp or a telegraph pole, to imagine oneself back in another century. The Calle del Pintor Aguiar (named after Gomera's most famous artistic son) leads into the Plaza de Leoncio Bento, in the middle of which is the church with its four domes built in the Moorish style. In the left-hand corner is the Ayuntamiento de Agulo, built in a pleasing colonial Spanish manner, with its cool green-and-white tiled floor figured to look like marble. In the streets behind the plaza balustraded balconies grace the front of decrepit stone houses. After looking round the town it is time to go and find a *tienda* or café selling the pastries for which Agulo is famed.

A Gomero who knows the island well summed up, in delightful broken English, the great difference in character between the people of the north and those of the south – a character largely moulded by climate: 'Peoples in Hermigua, Agulo, Vallehermoso very sad under cloud, but good writers and poets; peoples in south exuberant and funny.'

It was to the more fertile north that the conquistador families came in the early years of the Spanish occupation and social customs have always been more formal here. Here and in neighbouring Hermigua the local ruling landowners, the *casiques*, had their estates. Since the 1950s their almost feudal grip has been broken and there is now a burgeoning middle class. Certainly a neat little town like Agulo with such architectural refinement would be quite unthinkable in the south.

West doorway of the church in the Plaza de Leoncio Bento.

(LEFT AND RIGHT) *Street scene and houses in Agulo.*
(BELOW) *View over the town looking towards Tenerife.*

(LEFT) *A waterfall cascades down Bisquite after the winter rains.* (OPPOSITE) *The road from Las Rosas to Agulo winds its way down the* barranco.

The Hand of Man

*Natural materials and man-made artefacts
produce varied patterns and textures.*

HERMIGUA

Church bells by the convent.

Gateway into a courtyard.

The finest view of Hermigua is from the Carretera del Norte as it winds down to the sea from the Cumbre tunnel at El Rejo. In the deep valley below, white houses built two or three deep into the mountain line the long main street. Among the simple stone and plaster houses are several unexpectedly flamboyant 19th-century buildings, unmistakeably Spanish baroque in inspiration, with ornate balconies and decorated pediments: the yellow Palmarejo building is quite the best. By way of contrast, there is the calm of the 16th-century church and the convent on the valley side of the road.

Since the early 1900s much of Hermigua's wealth has been derived from the banana plantations which line the bottom of the valley. The first bananas grown here and sold in Northern Europe were the Canary 'Cavendish' type. Although sweeter, and for long preferred especially by the English, this smaller banana was ousted in the 1960s by the 'Gros Michelle' variety of Central America, a bigger and less tender fruit. Today, the sole export market for the sweet Canary banana is mainland Spain, and its future as a cash crop is in jeopardy.

In the middle of the town is Virgilio Brito's ethnographic museum of La Gomera. This is a private collection built up over many years, and it can be viewed by appointment. It includes old Chipude pottery made in a manner virtually unchanged for 5,000 years, and the woven wool and rag ponchos and rugs; grindstones; sheep- and goat-skin flour bags. Most striking of all is the primitive furniture consisting of three and four peg-legged stools, tables and benches low on the ground so that people could sit in comfort below the smoke from the fire in the single room which served as both kitchen and bedroom. The Europeans introduced iron tools in the 15th century, but in the remote villages they were only of the simplest kind; clearly an axe and a chisel were used to make this roughly hewn laurel-wood furniture. But to see the cunning mechanism of things like their mousetraps makes one realize how ingenious these Gomeros were with the few tools and the raw materials they had to hand: there is a lethal stone trap which would flatten any mouse lured underneath it; a thick rectangular slab of rock about 10 x 15 cm is propped at an angle on a triangular arrangement of pegs, and alongside a trip peg a piece of cheese is so placed that a mouse would be sure to dislodge it.

(OPPOSITE) *The town seen from the south, spreads out below the Carretera del Norte.*

The mountainsides of
Hermigua may be
steeper than those of
the south, but they are
much more fertile;
vines supported on a
lattice of bamboo thrive
here despite the cloud
which often sits like a
lid halfway up the val-
ley. On sunny days like
this (the photo shows
smoke from a bonfire,
not cloud) the terraces
stand out in sharp re-
lief on the mountain-
sides.
(OPPOSITE) *Hermigua,
looking towards
Tenerife.*

116

The Atlantic trade winds bring their lowering clouds over the central mountains, seen from Hermigua.

Everyday artefacts of the kind used by the Gomeros for hundreds of years: some of these – the baskets and the pottery – are still in use today.
(LEFT) *Winnowing forks with wool- and rag-woven blankets and a poncho.*
(RIGHT) *Lidded baskets, and examples of old pottery (once made at Chipude as well as at El Cercado) and wooden utensils.*

The pottery at El Cercado still carries on a tradition which stretches back into the remote past. The clay is shaped entirely by hand and when leather-hard is polished with a smooth basalt pebble; a few days later, it is polished again using the same stone and a finishing coat of red ochre is applied. The pots are placed in a wood-fired stone kiln and frequently come out marked with surface patches of blackened fire-shadow which add greatly to their charm. The shapes are traditional and each is designed for a specific use.

GARAJONAY NATIONAL PARK

An ancient legend tells the story of two young people, the beautiful Gara who falls in love with Jonay, a handsome boy who came to La Gomera from Tenerife on two inflated goat-skins. Gara's parents disapproved of their love and the young couple fled into the mountains pursued by the villagers. They climbed to the highest point of the island, where they sharpened the ends of two sticks, pointed them towards their chests and were pierced to death in a final embrace. The central mountain peak was named Garajonay after the luckless pair, and more recently has given its name to the National Park which now protects nearly 4,000 hectares of La Gomera's aboriginal sub-tropical rain forest. Roads and trails through the forest with barbecue and picnic sites (INSET, ABOVE) *make it easily accessible.*

The forest is predominantly of laurel, laurisilvia, *and tree heather,* fayal-brezal (INSET, BELOW), *but many other kinds of plants grow here too: a few are indigenous and of great interest to botanists, and some can be identified with fossils from the Sea of Tethys, the last vestige of which is the Mediterranean, following the splitting up of the land mass Pangaea some 200 million years ago to form the continents we know today. The forest is dependent on the moisture-bearing trade winds which constantly blow over the island from the north. Sometimes for days on end thick banks of chill clouds wreath the forest in their ghostly vapour and all is silent except for the relentless drip ... drip ... drip as moisture gathers on the trees and falls to the ground. This water builds up over underground basalt layers, where it is tapped by means of artesian wells and piped to the drier regions. Through*

aeons a deep layer of humus has built up, creating an unstable mixture of rock and soil; fierce winter storms cause landslips which strew the roads with trees and boulders. Without the forest, however, this rich soil would have been washed away and the island reduced to a barren rocky outcrop. The continuing presence of the rain forest guarantees the survival of the island's wonderfully varied landscape and its culture.

Aspects of the forest (ANTI-CLOCKWISE FROM TOP LEFT): *Rock and humus are the foundations of the forest.*
The long needles of the Canary pine are perfectly adapted to condense moisture from the clouds; it has been calculated that under these trees each square metre of ground receives the equivalent of 2,000 mm of rainfall per annum.
Tree heathers, with their papery white flowers, and thick-leaved laurels grow side by side; the former, even more than the Canary pine, is the great moisture gatherer – it condenses up to eight times more water than it needs for its own survival.
Beautiful white umbels stand out against the green of the forest.
(OPPOSITE) *Pine trees planted in the 1950s at the edge of the forest to prevent soil erosion.*

The mists covering the mountains cloak the trees with phantasmagorical lichens, and under the clouds even the palm trees lose their normal sunny exuberance.

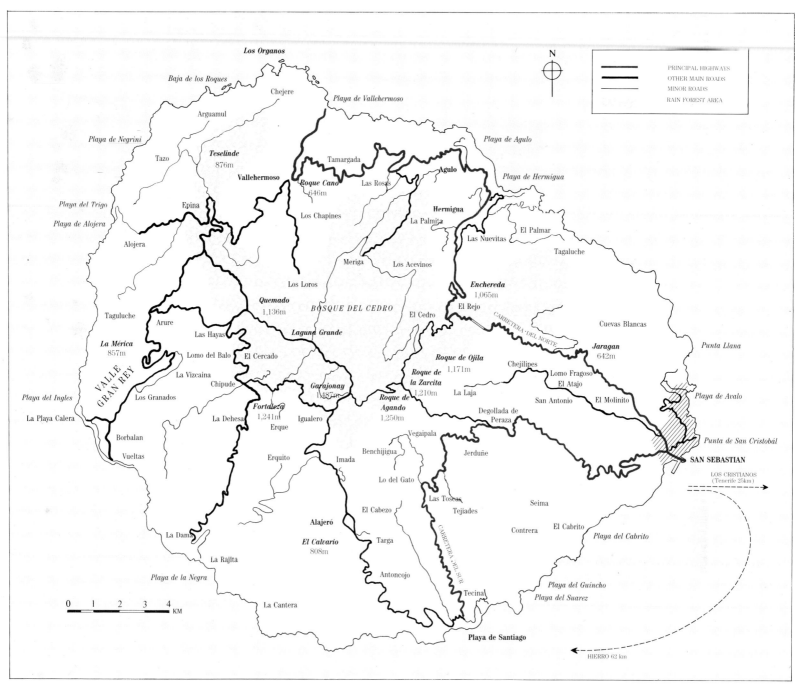

LA GOMERA

Map labels (place names, peaks, beaches, roads):

Los Organos
Baja de los Roques
Chejere
Playa de Vallehermoso
Arguamul
Teselinde 876m
Tamargada
Agulo
Playa de Agulo
Playa de Negrini
Tazo
Vallehermoso
Roque Cano 646m
Las Rosas
Playa de Hermigua
Playa del Trigo
Epina
Los Chapines
Hermigua
La Palmita
El Palmar
Playa de Alojera
Las Nuevitas
Tagaluche
Alojera
Meriga
Los Acevinos
Taguluche
Quemado 1,136m
BOSQUE DEL CEDRO
El Cedro
Enchereda 1,065m
El Rejo
Cuevas Blancas
La Mérica 857m
Arure
Las Hayas
Laguna Grande
El Cercado
Roque de Ojila 1,171m
Chejilipes
Lomo Fragoso
El Atajo
Jaragan 642m
Punta Llana
Lomo del Balo
La Vizcaina
Chipude
Garajonay 1,487m
Roque de la Zarcita 1,210m
La Laja
San Antonio
El Molinito
Playa de Avalo
Playa del Ingles
Los Granados
Fortaleza 1,241m
Igualero
Roque de Agando 1,250m
Degollada de Peraza
La Playa Calera
La Dehesa
Erque
Vegaipala
Punta de San Cristóbal
Borbalan
Erquito
Imada
Benchijigua
Jerduñe
SAN SEBASTIAN
Vueltas
Lo del Gato
Seima
La Dama
Las Toscas
El Cabezo
Tejiades
Contrera
El Cabrito
Playa del Cabrito
Alajeró
Targa
El Calvario 808m
Antoncojo
Tecina
Playa del Guincho
Playa del Suarez
La Rajlta
Playa de la Negra
La Cantera
Playa de Santiago

Los Chapines
Los Loros

VALLE GRAN REY

CARRETERA DEL NORTE
CARRETERA DEL SUR

LOS CRISTIANOS (Tenerife 25km)
HIERRO 62 km

0 1 2 3 4
KM

N

PRINCIPAL HIGHWAYS
OTHER MAIN ROADS
MINOR ROADS
RAIN FOREST AREA

ADMINISTRATIVE DIVISIONS

1 San Sebastián   4 Vallehermoso
2 Alajeró   5 Agulo
3 Valle Gran Rey   6 Hermigua

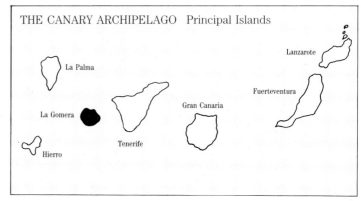

THE CANARY ARCHIPELAGO Principal Islands

La Palma
Lanzarote
Fuerteventura
La Gomera
Gran Canaria
Hierro
Tenerife